Cats: Little Tigers In Your House

by Linda McCarter Bridge
Photographs by Donna K. Grosvenor

BOOKS FOR YOUNG EXPLORERS
NATIONAL GEOGRAPHIC SOCIETY

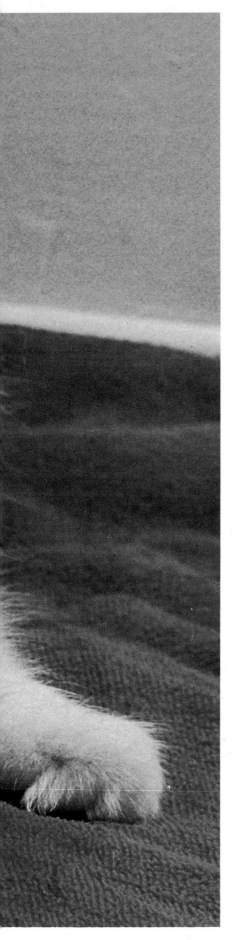

Something very special has just happened.
A little kitten has been born.
The mother rests after washing her new baby
with her tongue. Soon another baby is born.
Fezziwig is the mother of two kittens.
Kittens are born with their eyes shut tight.
Newborn kittens cannot see or hear,
but they can cry and purr.
They wobble around on tiny legs,
and they fall down again and again.

4

Fezziwig is a good mother.
She stays close to her kittens
in a cozy basket.
She puts a paw around her babies
and protects them while they sleep.
The kittens keep warm by snuggling
close to their mother.

When the kittens wake up, they are hungry.
They find their mother's nipples
and start sucking milk.
Even newborn kittens have sharp claws.
By the time the kittens are 8 days old,
their eyes begin to open, little by little.
When they are 11 days old,
their eyes are wide open.
A few days later the kittens begin to hear sounds.

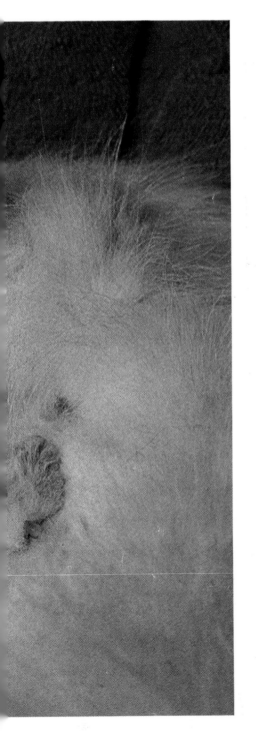

8 days old

10 days old

11 days old

Bath time! But the kitten named Toddly tries to squirm away. Fezziwig licks her kittens many times each day to keep them clean. After a bath, the family stretches out for a catnap.

Toddly swats Paddy Paws.
Paddy Paws hits Toddly right back.
Paddy Paws has white paws
and a white mark on his face.
Toddly jumps on Paddy Paws.
The kittens are about three weeks old,
and they are starting to fight and play.

Paddy Paws watches as Uncle Skeezix digs his claws into a scratching post. Some cats scratch at a post, and some cats climb it like a tree. In a few weeks, Toddly scrambles right up the post to the top. Later, Toddly plays with a toy tied to the post.

What do you think kittens do all day?
They bat at toys and a wooden duck.
They snoop in shoes. They climb
furniture, and curtains, and stairs.
They peek out from a fireplace screen
and from under a wicker table.
By the time Paddy Paws and Toddly
are a month old, they sniff and paw
things all over the house.
Cats are curious about many things.

Toby is a friendly dog, and he wants to come inside.
When Toby comes to meet the kittens,
Paddy Paws stands up, and spits and hisses at him.
Cats can also arch their backs and make their fur stand out.
Then they look bigger and scarier.
Later Toddly very carefully creeps close to Toby.

Lap, lap, lap.
Paddy Paws laps up dinner from a bowl.
After Toddly has eaten, he washes his leg.
The kittens have learned from their mother how to keep clean.

A cat's tongue is very important. It is used as a spoon
to drink milk or water. It is also used as a washcloth and brush.
Tiny bumps on the top of the tongue make it rough.
When a cat licks you, its tongue feels like sandpaper.

String is a favorite plaything. A kitten can tumble with it or pounce on it.

Toddly pokes his head out from his hiding place.
The kittens hide in baskets, boxes, and paper bags.
Paddy Paws is ready to pounce on Toddly.
The kittens roll over, and Toddly lands on top.
When kittens fight and play,
they are practicing to become good hunters.

String can be shared by two kittens. Or one kitten can get tangled up in it.

What a big yawn! Toddly grows tired playing
in a tipped-over wastebasket.
It is time for another nap.
Paddy Paws falls asleep on top of the sofa.
He looks like a fluffy powder puff.

The kittens sleep upstairs and downstairs.
They sleep on furniture and on the floor.
Sometimes they sleep alone,
and sometimes they cuddle close to each other.
Kittens sleep a lot.

Paddy Paws and Toddly
discover goldfish.
The kittens sit very still.
But their eyes follow
the bright fish swimming
in the fish tank.
When a fish swims near,
they swat at the tank
with a paw.
They are trying
to reach the fish
through the glass.
Even when kittens are small,
they try to hunt.

Toddly sees a moth on the window screen.
If Toddly moves very fast,
he might catch the moth. But this one flew away.
Paddy Paws watches Morris Mouse.
Morris lives in a glass cage, safe from the kittens.
When Morris runs around in the cage,
they always bat at the glass with their paws.
As kittens grow up, they will hunt mice,
and birds, and other small creatures, whenever they can.
House cats are related to lions and tigers,
and they hunt in the same ways these big cats do.

Ssshh! Two fuzzy hunters creep on padded paws through the garden.
They are stalking a bug.
Suddenly they run across the grass to chase something else.

Meow! Meow!
Paddy Paws jumped
into a big flowerpot,
and he can't get out.
Kittens make a lot of noise
when they are scared.

Cats are good climbers.
When they climb up a tree,
cats dig their claws into the bark.

Now the kittens are two months old, and they are ready to go
to their new home. Sam and Dana come over to learn how to take care of
their new pets. Dana hugs Paddy Paws, and, later, Sam plays with him.

The children are ready to take the kittens home.
Sam puts Paddy Paws into a cardboard box.
Toddly sticks his head out through a hole in the box.
As the children pull the wagon away, Toddly peeks out,
as if to say good-bye. The children are very happy.
Paddy Paws and Toddly will be playful, cuddly pets
even after they have grown into big, beautiful cats.

These pictures of the kittens show how their faces change as they grow from the day of birth to the age of two months.

3 hours   6 days   11 days

15 days   21 days   24 days   30 days   36 days

42 days   45 days   51 days   55 days   59 days

Published by The National Geographic Society
Melvin M. Payne, *President;* Melville Bell Grosvenor, *Editor-in-Chief;*
Gilbert M. Grosvenor, *Editor.*

Prepared by
The Special Publications Division
Robert L. Breeden, *Editor*
Donald J. Crump, *Associate Editor*
Philip B. Silcott, *Senior Editor*
Cynthia Russ Ramsay, *Managing Editor*
Toni Eugene, *Research*

Illustrations, Design and Art Direction
Donald J. Crump, *Picture Editor*
Joseph A. Taney, *Staff Art Director,* Ursula Perrin, *Designer*
Jane D'Alelio, Sara Grosvenor, *Design Assistants*

Production and Printing
Robert W. Messer, *Production Manager*
George V. White, *Assistant Production Manager*
Raja D. Murshed, Nancy W. Glaser, *Production Assistants*
John R. Metcalfe, *Engraving and Printing*
Mary G. Burns, Jane H. Buxton, Marta Isabel Coons,
    Suzanne J. Jacobson, Marilyn L. Wilbur, *Staff Assistants*

Consultants
Dr. Glenn O. Blough, *Educational Consultant*
Dr. Gordon S. Davis and Dr. William D. Swartz, *Veterinarians;*
    Dr. Henry W. Setzer, *Curator, Division of Mammals,*
    Smithsonian Institution, Washington, D.C.; Scientific Consultants
Edith K. Chasnov, Lynn Z. Lang, *Reading Specialists*